Engaging the Team at Zingerman's Mail Order

After decades of implementing Lean tools, organizations are getting serious about the heart and soul of Lean management. They are developing people to continuously improve. Most of the Lean tools, such as kanban, andon, and visual management, are designed to surface problems so you know what to work on to achieve your goal. Engaged, scientific-thinking team members solve them one by one.

Toyota's underlying assumption is that the world is complex and uncertain, and we never have the perfect solution, so whatever is implemented needs continual refinement as we learn and as the marketplace changes. If we can't predict what is around the corner, then a key skill is being able to learn and to adapt to what appears. *Where do we want to go? How can we ensure that everyone contributes to our journey?*

This book builds on *Lean in a High-Variability Business*. It is a shorter, focused introduction to developing scientific thinking through deliberate practice with Toyota Kata (TK). TK has practice routines ('Starter Kata') for both the learner trying to change how they approach problems to a more systematic, scientific approach, and the coach trying to teach them by helping them work toward actual goals. The focus is on the HOW of developing engaged managers and supervisors who in turn can develop an engaged workforce. There are many books about why engagement is important and descriptions of best practices, but few provide practical guidance on how to actually achieve it. And there are none in an easy-to-understand comic or graphic form.

It is only through deliberate practice that we can develop a new, habitual way of thinking to avoid jumping to conclusions and let the facts and evidence guide us. Here's how one organization does it. You can too.

Engaging the Team at Zingerman's Mail Order

A Toyota Kata Comic

Eduardo Lander
Jeffrey K. Liker
Tom Root

Illustrations by Jazmín Morales

Routledge
Taylor & Francis Group

A PRODUCTIVITY PRESS BOOK
COMIC

First published 2024
by Routledge
605 Third Avenue, New York, NY 10158

and by Routledge
4 Park Square, Milton Park, Abingdon, Oxon, OX14 4RN

Routledge is an imprint of the Taylor & Francis Group, an informa business

ISBN: 978-1-032-44536-6 (hbk)
ISBN: 978-1-032-44535-9 (pbk)
ISBN: 978-1-003-37265-3 (ebk)

DOI: 10.4324/9781003372653

Typeset in Comic Sans
by codeMantra

Publisher's note: This book has been prepared from camera-ready copy provided by the authors.

Engaging the Team
at ZINGERMAN'S MAIL ORDER

Zingerman's deli was founded in 1982 to bring high-quality artisanal food to Ann Arbor, Michigan.

Zingerman's Mail Order brings those foods everywhere in the USA!

Zingerman's Mail Order (ZMO) is a spin-off of the Zingerman's delicatessen. It's a call center + a receiving/packing/shipping warehouse + team members who work to provide customers the best possible experience.

Zingerman's is famous for its people-oriented culture using servant leadership. ZMO also practiced Toyota Kata, to mobilize scientific-thinking capability and turn each team member into a partner in the daily struggle to learn and adapt.

Here's your ringside seat to how ZMO met the goal of engaging its team.

Partner — TOM

Over the years we had remarkable success utilizing Lean techniques to continually improve our work processes, creating a fairly smooth, efficient and effective workflow despite being in an unpredictable high-variety business. Every year companies visit ZMO to see how we do it. However, those improvements were initiated and developed by a small group of senior managers, myself included. We still had nagging problems every day and we needed help solving them. We needed to engage everyone's brain, but so far had failed.

Manager — BETTY

Exactly! Improvement was something done by management, who tried to push others to do it. But there was no appeal for the front liners, and no ownership. People preferred to have their teeth pulled rather than participate in continuous improvement!

Advisor — EDUARDO

As the outside advisor to ZMO on their lean journey I'm proud of what the management team accomplished and learned. But we tried different approaches to involve front liners without success, until we began experimenting with Toyota Kata. What is TK and how did it help us engage team members? Read on!

Cast of Characters

Eduardo	Betty	Mo	Lisa	Tom	"J"	Prof. Liker
Advisor	Manager	Partner	Manager	Partner	Manager	Advisor

And the ZMO crew!

A breakthrough in the Lean movement came with a book by Womack and Jones called Lean Thinking. They said Lean is a way of <u>thinking</u> about maximizing value to the customer while minimizing waste. This shifts the focus from the Lean tools to the people in the organization.

Hmmm... I think I get what you're saying. The people doing the work know the work the best. They feel the daily problems firsthand and know when something is broken. We need their help to improve, so we can more efficiently provide better service to our customers.

That's very exciting! It is the core of our philosophy at Zingerman's. We believe in a kind of workplace democracy. We want everyone involved in improving so we can provide a better service to our customers every day.

Previously...
Having the 'Culture' Conversation

Eduardo, I keep going back to your comment about developing the process, people and culture. Seems like a lot to bite off at the same time.

Culture?
People ↔ Process

Couldn't we start with one? Maybe culture, to prepare the people?

Dr. Liker has taught me to start with the process but engage the people right away. Over time, the culture will evolve through repeated experience. Just telling people what the new culture should be doesn't do much. But changing behaviors changes how people think. This changes the culture!

Process
Culture ↔ People

If we don't have this parallel development on all fronts, then the improvements we make probably won't be sustained... and they will certainly not continue to evolve in the future.

So we focus on the process, and that drags the rest along?

More or less. But the key is to involve people early in solving problems. This develops the way they think, which in turn evolves the culture. And of course, you have the leadership team, who has to model and continually reinforce the new culture.

MATURITY

PLAN

CONTINUOUS IMPROVEMENT FOR LONG TERM SUCCESS

ACT

PROCESS PEOPLE

CHECK

TIME

Ok... parallel process and people development. Culture follows. Sounds like a plan.

TOM

That much we got – the theory. But making it work was another story.

Through the years, Lean was always led by top management, but we wanted to involve the whole crew. Our first attempt to engage a wider group was based on 'PDCA' – Plan, Do, Check, Act – and 5-whys. It utterly failed! All our preaching about PDCA and asking lots of whys left our team members cold. Minimum involvement. No engagement. No behavior change.

We then had the idea to **pay for experiments,** and proposed a system expressly designed to bypass top management and motivate the wider ZMO community. Let's take a look at how that worked out.

"That would increase focus on our priorities. Interesting..."

"Exactly! Now, we are thinking of tying the reward to running experiments that could improve a Standard Operating Procedure (SOP). In the end, people would get paid whether they manage to improve or not."

"We want to encourage the crew to experiment, but we do not want to penalize them if their idea does not work as planned. More experiments should result in more improvements."

"Did it work?"

"Hmm... guess not."

"Yes!"

Reward

Reward

"I get that, but how does the process work? If someone has an idea, they run an experiment and then come get their reward?"

"Well, we need a bit more structure, both to support people so they learn from the experiment, and to ensure we reward them fairly."

"First, there are some pre-requisites. People need to attend the 'How to Teach' and 'How to Plan and Conduct an Experiment' classes. We'll track those in their Zingerman's training passports."

1. Attend classes
2. Apply for grant → area and SOP

"Then, they need to apply for the grant by explaining to one of the counselors... initially me... which area they want to work on and which SOP they will try to improve."

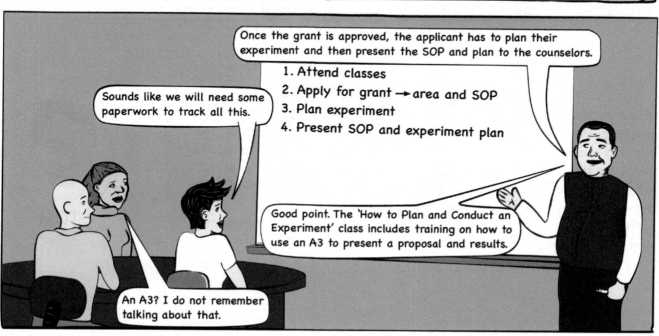

"Once the grant is approved, the applicant has to plan their experiment and then present the SOP and plan to the counselors."

1. Attend classes
2. Apply for grant → area and SOP
3. Plan experiment
4. Present SOP and experiment plan

"Sounds like we will need some paperwork to track all this."

"Good point. The 'How to Plan and Conduct an Experiment' class includes training on how to use an A3 to present a proposal and results."

"An A3? I do not remember talking about that."

Name	Date	Experimental Plan (resources and process)
Area		
Question		
Background Research		Results
Hypothesis		Conclusion

A3 is a standard paper size. In Toyota, it refers to summarizing your ideas on one side of one document, so everything is visible at a glance.

Once the counselor certifies the SOP and plan, the applicant can proceed with the experiment. They get the reward once completed.

1. Attend classes
2. Apply for grant → area and SOP
3. Plan experiment
4. Present SOP and experiment
5. Run experiment
6. Get reward

It seems to me that if things go well, we will need multiple counselors.

Yes, we will. When we launch, I will open applications for the first three counselor positions, with a cash reward for advising grant awardees.

What does it take to become a counselor?

They need to take the classes and go through one CI grant process with me as counselor.

Sounds like you have all angles covered. When do we launch it?

I was thinking we could explain it in the huddle next week and schedule the first class for the week after. We can start taking CI Grant applications immediately after that.

You may be wondering how this went. Terribly! Few people got involved. We thought that maybe it was not enough money, or the process was too cumbersome, or that we expected them to do the work on their own time. The truth is we never found out exactly why, but it was clear the experiment failed. So we continued with top-driven improvements, trying to involve people early. Unfortunately, they mostly wanted to follow our lead, not propose and drive improvements on their own.

TOM

Experiment 3: Toyota Business Practices

Hello! How are you? How are things going in Brussels?

All fine here... but after five good years of learning at Toyota, I've decided to move on. Now I'm thinking of sharing what I've learned with small companies. I really enjoyed the work we did together. Would you be interested in more support?

Brussels Ann Arbor

Are you kidding? That would be great!

Good! It won't be as easy as when I lived 5 minutes away, but I think we can make it work.

TOM

That was October 2012. Eduardo left Toyota in early December and came to visit during our Christmas peak.

Since then, we have been working with him again. But let's go back to our story. So far, we had failed twice at engaging our associates in continuous improvement, and now Eduardo brought from Toyota our third attempt, which we started early in 2013. Let's see how that went...

EDUARDO

I'm glad to see a lot has changed since I was last here. I see many improvements to the layout and workstations. I particularly like the effort that has gone into SOPs. I see them everywhere in the warehouse, and people mostly follow them. Plus, every discussion about the process starts with the SOP. That's a great foundation for continuous improvement.

Yes, but we're still driving improvement from the top. This group here, plus the partners, generate the bulk of ideas and push them through.

And we're still the bottleneck. We get a lot done on big issues, but we still miss a lot of the small improvements. I suspect that if we added those up, they would amount to at least the same benefits as the big improvements we drive top-down.

Large improvements

Small improvements

Hmm... sounds like we need to involve more people. In that you're not different than Toyota. Even today, they continue to work hard at engaging people. When I worked there, they were rolling out the latest program to coach people on problem solving. They call it Toyota Business Practices.

Another problem-solving methodology? Do you think that's what we need?

At Toyota TBP is more than a problem-solving methodology. The vision is for it to be how everyone practices the Toyota Way in their daily activities. Thus the name. They want continuous improvement to be a way of life.

But to answer your question... I'm not sure if TBP is the right solution for ZMO. I do know it works very well for Toyota and I also know that without trying, we won't know if it works here.

Don't worry, J, you will get used to his cryptic answers.

Cryptic? I am a down-to-earth guy. Anyway, to get wide participation in continuous improvement, several elements must come together. Remember our discussion about a safe environment where people can make mistakes? Well, a structured problem-solving methodology is another one of these elements.

Tell us more about this TBP.

Ok, the problem-solving side of TBP...

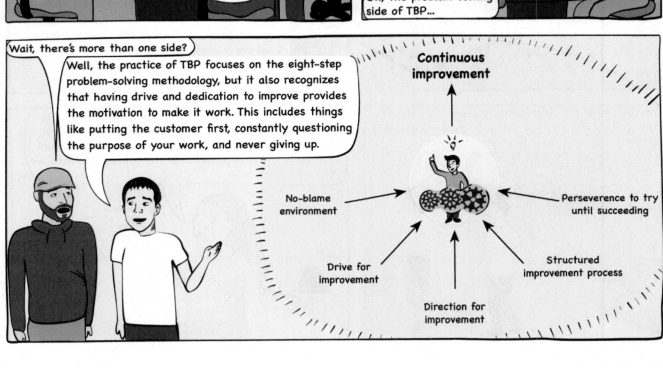

Wait, there's more than one side?

Well, the practice of TBP focuses on the eight-step problem-solving methodology, but it also recognizes that having drive and dedication to improve provides the motivation to make it work. This includes things like putting the customer first, constantly questioning the purpose of your work, and never giving up.

Continuous improvement

No-blame environment

Drive for improvement

Direction for improvement

Structured improvement process

Perseverence to try until succeeding

What do you mean by smaller problems? I thought the gap was the problem we need to solve.

The gap to the ideal state is typically too big as a starting point. There are many issues we'll need to tackle to solve it, so we break the big problem into smaller sub problems and select the most promising one. For example, a subproblem we could start with is the crew's lack of training in TBP.

Let me try... If our prioritized problem is lack of training, maybe a target could be for half the crew to do one TBP project by the end of the year. How's that?

Great. You can use it to measure progress and evaluate overall results at the end of the year... both needed in a good target.

That would be challenging, but I see what you mean. What's next?

Got it, but we have struggled with this. We usually end up with too many causes.

And it's hard to know when to stop...

We'll have to practice. In general, we want to start with a wide range of possible causes and then confirm or discard each through direct analysis of the facts at the process, before moving on to the next level.

Hmm... makes sense, when you put it that way. What's next?

To set a target for the prioritized problem we selected. A target should be challenging, measurable, and concrete... and have a deadline.

1. Clarify the problem
2. Break down the problem
3. Set a target

Ideal condition

Target

Prior...

Current cond...

Gap = Problem

Ok... the next step is to find the root cause of the problem. Focusing on the prioritized problem, we're going to ask 'why' multiple times, going deeper, until we find the root cause. Without it, it will be hard to solve the problem for good.

1. Clarify the problem
2. Break down the problem
3. Set a target
4. Analyze the root cause

Ideal condition

Target

Gap = Problem

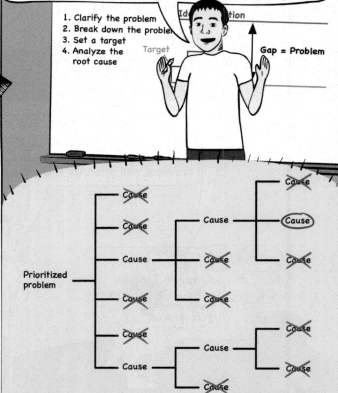

Prioritized problem

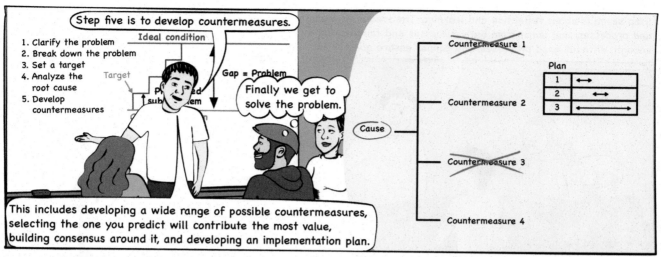

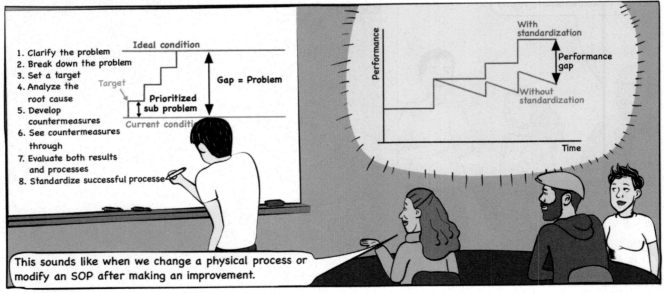

What about this one? How do you think that went? Worse than terribly! We spent about three months in weekly video conferences with Eduardo trying to use it. We tackled a couple of problems, but only with the management team, and in the second one we did not even make it past the root cause analysis. It felt complex and cumbersome, taking too much time and effort to get to the same result we would have reached with our much less structured observation and discussion approach. It did not fit our action-oriented people and culture. Back to square one... now what?

TOM

PDCA & 5-whys ~~(crossed out)~~

Improvement grants ~~(crossed out)~~

TBP ~~(crossed out)~~

???

So, we tried TBP and it doesn't seem quite right for ZMO.

My head is still spinning from TBP. Glad to move on from that!!

It was a struggle, even with your help. I don't think we could have used it effectively with the crew.

Please don't tell me it's another problem-solving methodology.

Not really. The focus is on developing thinking patterns. By using a structured approach to work towards challenging goals, people develop the ability to think scientifically, and that helps with any problem-solving method. A few elements could make it a good fit for ZMO.

Well, to be honest, Toyota uses TBP mostly for management, not frontline workers. It is for longer-term challenges, not so much for the day-to-day problems warehouse associates face. We still need to find the right approach for ZMO... something more intuitive.

I'll bite... any ideas?

Well, there's a book called Toyota Kata, written by Mike Rother. He was also a graduate student of Dr. Liker and lives here in Ann Arbor. In fact, he showed me all the mountain bike trails around town. The book is about developing scientific thinking so people can work toward a big goal in small bite-sized steps.

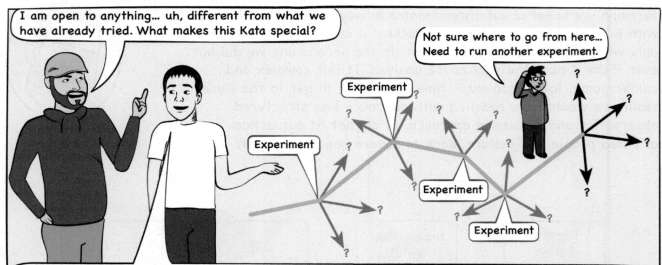

I am open to anything... uh, different from what we have already tried. What makes this Kata special?

Not sure where to go from here... Need to run another experiment.

Experiment

Experiment

Experiment

Experiment

Well, the scientific thinking model, which Mike calls the Improvement Kata, is simple and has a strong bias for action. Where TBP can lead to a great deal of evaluation and planning, resulting in several countermeasures which are then implemented rapidly, Kata focuses on finding your way through simple and inexpensive experiments.

So Toyota Kata is a sequence of activities to teach us how to think?

How to think scientifically, yes. Mike developed a kata for improvement and another for coaching. He calls them starter kata because they help us learn the fundamentals. Mike is less interested in theoretical learning than in the mindset... the way we think about reaching goals.

Before we go much deeper... I learned a lot more about TBP when we started using it. Can we go there directly? Can we use Kata to learn how to use Kata?

Kata the Kata

Now you're twisting my brain.

Hmm... interesting idea. Let's give it a try.

But how do we start without any experience?

It seems similar enough to what I learned at Toyota. I think I can get us started.

Ok, where do we begin?

With the end.

Now you're really trying to confuse us.

Not at all. The first step in the Improvement Kata is to understand the direction. What do we want to achieve? Okada-san, my Japanese coordinator at Toyota, started every new activity, big or small, by asking: what's the end image?

IMPROVEMENT KATA

1

Set the Direction or Challenge

I'm a bit slow, so it took a while to understand what he meant and why it was so important. What he wanted was to define what we needed to achieve... to create a clear image of what success would look like.

Hmm... in a weird way that, makes sense. Sounds like what we call 'visioning' at Zingerman's.

You're moving fast, J! What you just did took me about a year to figure out. I guess I'm done, you can take over now.

I said it kind of makes sense, but I don't know what to do with it, so you're not off the hook yet.

Fair point. We'll figure it out soon. Now, what does success look like with respect to using Kata?

For years, we have been trying to get wide participation in continuous improvement, so everyone makes their processes better every day, and ZMO benefits through the accumulation of many small steps. As management, we focus on the big picture and frequently miss opportunities hidden in the details of each process.

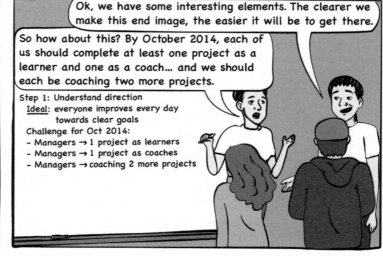

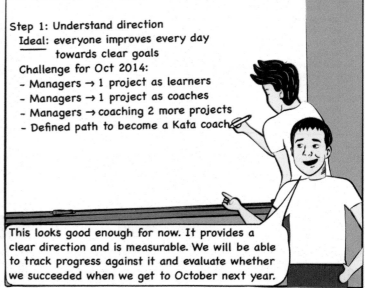

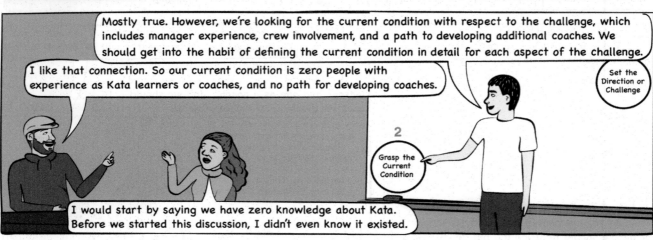

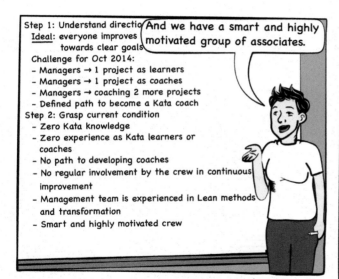

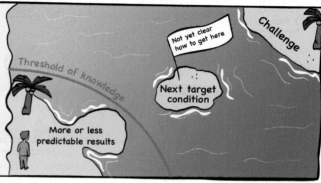

The final step is to experiment to reach the target condition. We have to identify obstacles preventing us from operating as described by the target condition, choose one, propose actions to overcome it, and try one of those out.

We can go do something already? You were not joking when you said this was action oriented.

IMPROVEMENT KATA

1 Set the Direction or Challenge

3 Establish your Next Target Condition

2 Grasp the Current Condition

4 Conduct Experiments to get there

Well, different problems require different levels of analysis. Normally, grasping the current condition requires more study, but in general, we want quick cycles of learning. Once you reach your threshold of knowledge, go try something out and learn. Don't delay... think about what you can start today or tomorrow.

I like it!

Current condition · Experiments · Obstacles · Next target condition · Challenge

Strong connections in a logically sound story

One thing, though... do not confuse the bias for action with a lack of rigor. The challenge, current condition, next target condition, obstacles preventing us from reaching it, and experiments we run are all part of a story that has to be logically sound. Stronger connections result in more learning and better improvements.

We'll have to see how that works, but it kind of makes sense. What's next?

Next, I need to catch a flight, and you need to think about your main obstacles. But let me jump ahead a bit and ask you to spend the next few days studying. First, go to Mike's website. It has a great YouTube lecture. And of course, get the Toyota Kata book.

We can do that. Enjoy your flight while we go back to school.

A couple of weeks later, Betty gets a call from Jeff.

Hi Betty, this is Jeff Liker. We know each other mostly through Eduardo Lander. I have a big request.

Hi Jeff. Great to hear from you. We can do big requests. What did you have in mind?

I am teaching a new Lean graduate course that includes projects based on something pretty new, Toyota Kata. I was hoping my students could work with your team at ZMO on some of these projects. Can we meet, maybe even this afternoon?

Wow, believe it or not, we just started learning about Toyota Kata. I would love to talk more about it. Come on over.

Hi, Jeff, let's go to my office and discuss this kata stuff. I've asked my co-managers Lisa and J to join us.

Before we start, let me thank you on behalf of ZMO for all you have done for us through Eduardo. He has been a life saver.

I can't take a lot of credit for him. As you probably have learned, he has a mind of his own.

Well, thank you anyway. I still can't believe you're here to talk about Kata. My number one objective this year is to start using it. Can you believe that?

That's great! Kata is pretty new for me as well. Sounds like we can learn together.

That would be amazing. These are Lisa and J. You both know Jeff Liker. Now that we're all here, tell us more about this class of yours, Jeff. It sounds very interesting.

Hi. The class is mostly for master's students in industrial engineering, and I want it to have a strong practical component. Students will learn concepts in the classroom and then go out into companies to apply them. We'll be teaching the students how to tackle challenging goals through scientific thinking. In their projects here, I would love for them to work side by side with your people on meaningful issues. We expect a lot of learning in both directions.

PARTNERSHIP FOR LEARNING

UM   ZMO

Sounds too good to be true. Can you tell us more about how you will teach students about scientific thinking?

Well, in the class we cover Lean principles so they can apply them in their projects, but the main thread of the course is based on Toyota Kata. It's similar to what Toyota uses to develop people internally but was specifically designed by Mike Rother to help other organizations develop scientific thinking skills, without having to be immersed in a culture where it's the norm.

This is an incredible coincidence.

Isn't it? I was telling Jeff we just started learning about Kata.

Yes, our last meeting with Eduardo focused on defining our next attempt at engaging a wider group in continuous improvement. We even started using Kata to learn about Kata.

What do you mean?

Jeff, going back to your class... how do you envision this working? We and the students will all be learning. Who's the learner and who's the coach?

I don't have all the answers, but the good thing about Kata is that we don't have to know everything in advance. This class is an experiment. We will learn and improve it for next year. My image is that small groups of say, three students team up with a few of your people to learn together, step-by-step working on real projects. I want the students to start in the learner role, but they may evolve quickly into coaches.

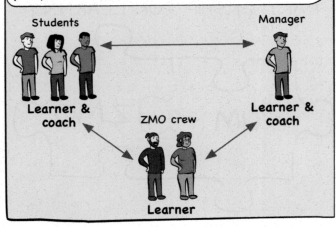

Well, we defined a challenge, our current condition, and the first target condition. We're now identifying obstacles so we can start our first experiment.

That's great. It seems my timing is impeccable, or at least really lucky.

If a lot of learning happens in the classroom, could ZMO team members involved attend the class at the University of Michigan?

I had not thought about that. It would ensure everyone has a common understanding of Kata. Good idea! Don't tell my boss though.

Starting the second week of January, we had eight teams of students roaming around the warehouse. Each team was paired with a couple of frontline crew members and supported by a manager. They met regularly and scheduled experiments as needed, but the students also dropped in at any time just to observe the process. And our associates took a graduate course at UM! They were intimidated at first, but ended up loving the experience.

Results? Amazing! Well beyond expectations. It's true the first year was a bit hectic. Nobody had any real experience with Kata, so the students and crew tried to learn together as they ran the projects. The difference between teams was huge in both the approach and the results. Some jumped right in to make changes without understanding the current condition or how they would measure success, while others analyzed the data to death and beyond. And evolving to become a coach was much harder than expected. However, for participants and ZMO in general, **it was a transformative experience that resulted in huge engagement in improvement efforts.** There was a newfound enthusiasm to try ideas out and experiment.

It was almost like flipping a switch. We went from almost no involvement to electrifying participation in a matter of months.

BETTY

Tom says it well. As I mentioned, before Kata our people preferred getting a tooth pulled to participating in improvement activities. After running a few Kata projects, we had to turn people away because we did not (yet) have enough experienced coaches to support so many projects simutaneously.

Involvement did a 180 at ZMO. Practicing Toyota Kata is creating a continuous improvement culture, and we continue to expand new Kata activities into different departments.

Comments from the ZMO Crew

"I like problem solving... and this process has visuals that show progress clearly. Besides, fewer stock-outs means less work for me."

"It directly impacts the work at my station... reduces workload. I have freedom to make changes. It seems to fit well with my background."

"You get to think and use your brain!"

"I like the idea of improving a process and moving it forward."

"I'm naturally organized, so TK seems logical... it's common sense. I like being involved, and with this I can control changes and see progress. It's very visual. It allows me to talk on the same level to anyone in the organization."

"I like fixing things and I'm detailed oriented, but I frequently don't know where to start. The kata gives me a clear process and direction."

We've looked at how Toyota Kata helped us engage people. Now let's look at how TK actually works, by going through a student project on bread preparation. Since Kata is new to the students, we followed Mike's Starter Kata for beginners rigorously. As your scientific-thinking skills grow you may develop your own way, to match the needs of your organization. At ZMO we have made some changes to the Kata practice routines to fit our context.

TOM

Over the next years, the partnership with the University of Michigan continued to bring students to ZMO during the winter term. As the managers and crew gained practice, they provided a better learning experience for students. The managers have become highly skilled coaches, allowing students to focus on the learner role. Here Betty is coaching.

Hello everyone and welcome to bread. I'm Betty, and I'll be the coach for this Kata project. From ZMO we also have the bread captains Tess and Mike J. And from UM, we have Krati, Navish, Arjun, and Ganesh.

Arjun | Ganesh | Tess | Mike J. | Krati | Navish

Let's start with a bit of background. Last Christmas the bread area could not keep up, and now we have to go even faster. We have forecasted that bread will need to process one loaf every 7.5 seconds for the 2016 holiday season. You know that as 'takt'.

I was wondering about the rate of customer demand. Sounds like we have our challenge! Prepare one loaf every 7.5 seconds to ensure the line has bread when needed.

Wow, you jumped right into that. And of course, the challenge comes with the usual restrictions: minimum investment, no additional footprint, no additional people.

Those are some tight limitations.

Well, the challenge should be... challenging. We want it to be well beyond what Mike Rother calls our threshold of knowledge.

Don't worry, it's way beyond mine.

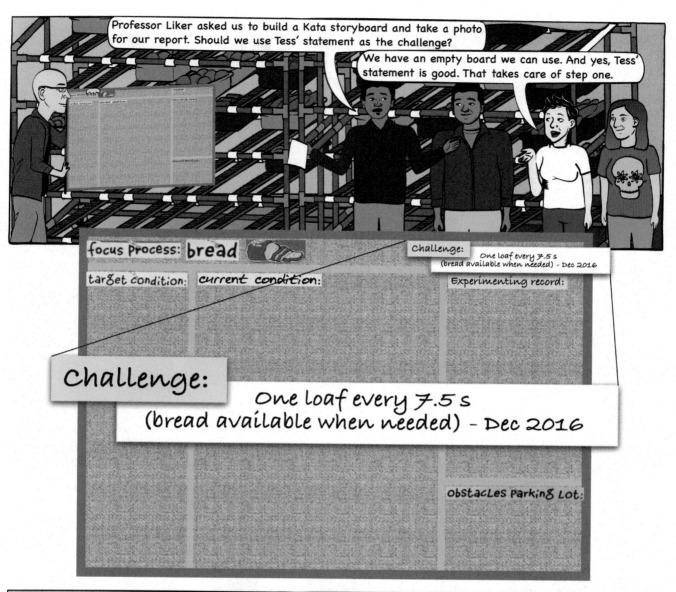

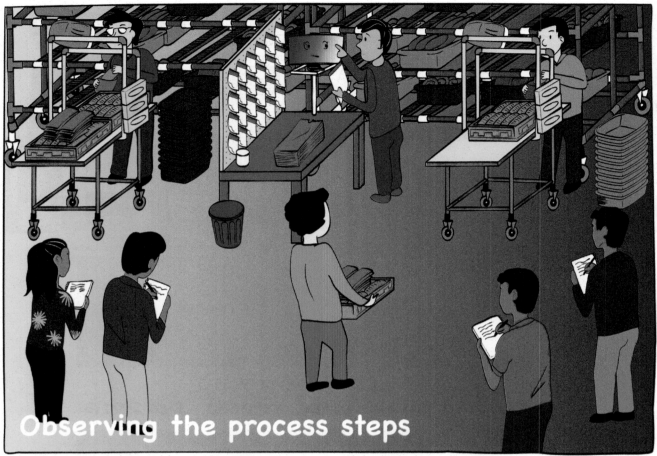

Observing the process steps

30 minutes later

Ok, let's discuss briefly where we are. What have we learned so far?

Well, the process here consists of taking naked bread, bagging it, and putting it in totes in the market.

That's mostly the case, but sometimes the bread comes in plastic bags... and others it needs to be sliced.

The bread in plastic bags comes from the freezer. We use that when we do not have enough coming from the Bakehouse. Slicing is a special request from customers.

I saw three distinct jobs. A person takes the totes from the line and prepares paper bags with labels for the breads needed, another moves the bread to where it will be bagged, and two people bag it.

That's right. We call the first Dispatch. They use signals from the line called kanban, to tell them how many bags are needed.

A key point here is that the number of bags matches the number of loaves that should go into the tote.

Right. The second job is the Taxi Driver. This person receives the labeled bags, gets the corresponding bread, and delivers both to the correct bagging station. Finally, the Baggers bag the bread and place it in the market behind them.

Sorry, how many different breads do you have?

It may change with the season, but right now we have 36 types.

Another question... I see four bagging stations, but only two in use. Are the others for the holiday peak?

Yes, the number of people matches the expected demand. On slower days, you may see only two people doing all three jobs. On faster days, all four bagging stations get used.

These great observations and questions give us a general sense of the operation. As a next step, we want to understand the current work pattern and the performance it implies in relation to our challenge. What else should we look for?

We learned in class to time each process multiple times and plot it on what is called a Run Chart. Then we can see the ups and downs and how it compares to takt time.

Professor Liker says that this is similar to how Toyota teaches by asking the learner to stand in a circle and just observe the processes to develop a deep understanding.

Interesting. Making a run chart not only provides a structure for observing the current condition, but it also forces you to observe deeply.

We also learned about an Operator Balance Chart. This compares the time each person takes to do their job to the rate of customer demand. Can they keep up? Is there waiting time?

Good point... should we try that now?

Sure. We should time cycles of work to develop the run chart. If I recall, ten cycles is a good number to start with.

First, let's agree on how to do this. I see that each job is done in a batch, but the number of loaves changes depending on the type of bread.

It does. Mostly depending on the usual sales volume for the specific bread.

Got it. Then, I think our metric should be time per loaf. This means we should record the time and number of loaves in each batch.

That's a very good insight. We need a common way of comparing across jobs and bread types. We also need to compare our findings to the challenge, which is given in seconds per loaf.

This is exciting! Let's get some timings and create these run charts.

Timing work cycles

30 min later

Let's get back together. How did it go? Do we have data already?

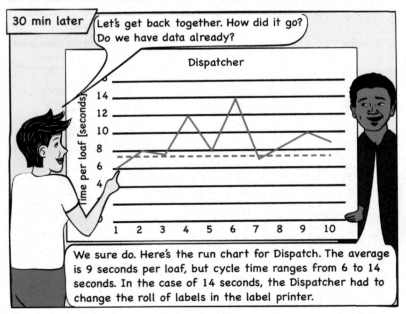

Dispatcher

Time per loaf (seconds)

We sure do. Here's the run chart for Dispatch. The average is 9 seconds per loaf, but cycle time ranges from 6 to 14 seconds. In the case of 14 seconds, the Dispatcher had to change the roll of labels in the label printer.

Mine is much faster. I have 3.5 seconds per loaf for the Taxi Driver, with a range from 2 to 5 seconds. In the longest two cycles new bread coming into the area was in the way and had to be moved.

Baggers are the slowest. Combining Navish's timings and mine, we get an average of 37.2 seconds, ranging from 28 to 54. The slowest times were for frozen bread.

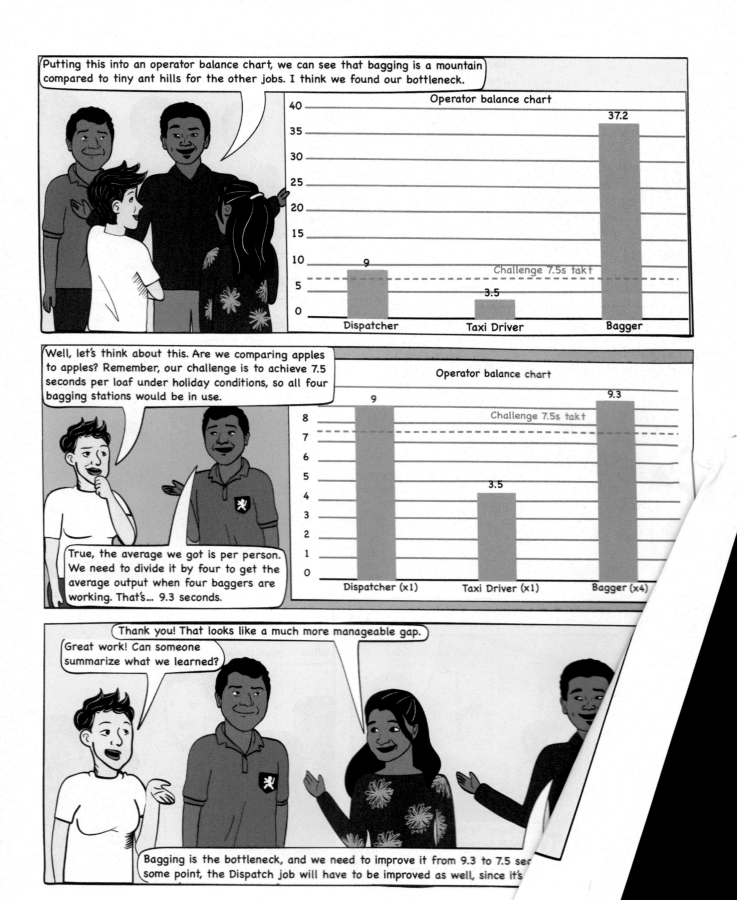

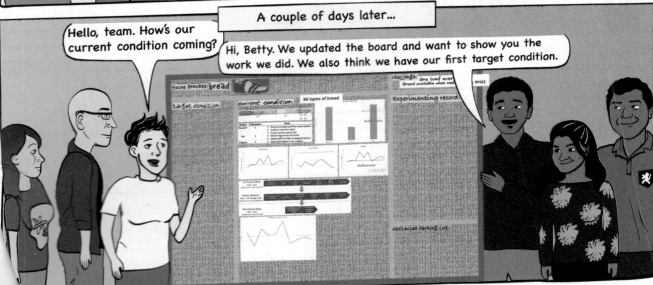

COACHING KATA

The Five Questions

① What is the **Target Condition**?

② What is the **Actual Condition** now?

--------(Turn Card Over)------------>

③ What **Obstacles** do you think are preventing you from reaching the target condition? Which *one* are you addressing now?

④ What is your **Next Step**? (Next experiment) What do you expect?

⑤ How quickly can we go and see what we **Have Learned** from taking that step?

*You'll often work on the same obstacle with several experiments

Oh, yes... Professor Liker emphasized that the target condition includes the desired outcome, in this case 10 seconds, and also the desired process condition. He mentioned that this is like taking a time machine to see how the process will look in two weeks.

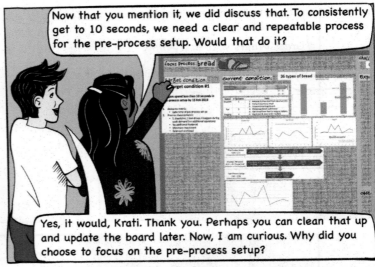

Now that you mention it, we did discuss that. To consistently get to 10 seconds, we need a clear and repeatable process for the pre-process setup. Would that do it?

Yes, it would, Krati. Thank you. Perhaps you can clean that up and update the board later. Now, I am curious. Why did you choose to focus on the pre-process setup?

Our timings show that bagging is the bottleneck...

Which matches what we see during the holidays. When we bring people in to help, they usually go to bagging.

In addition, we can break the baggers' activities into three blocks: pre-process setup, bagging process, and post-process setup.

That's the process steps diagram we have on the board.

You are on a roll! Keep going.

We chose to start with the pre-process setup because we see clear opportunities for improvement there.

I love your reasoning. There's a clear logic to your story, and it's well documented on the board.

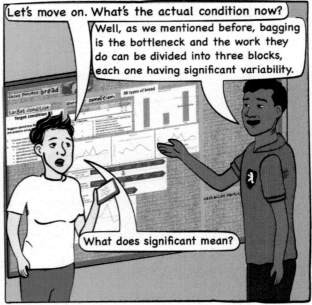

Let's move on. What's the actual condition now?

Well, as we mentioned before, bagging is the bottleneck and the work they do can be divided into three blocks, each one having significant variability.

What does significant mean?

As you can see on the run chart, it can take between 5.6 and 17 seconds per loaf.

That is definitely significant... When you give me numbers, or even better, show me a chart, there's a higher chance we end up with the same understanding of the situation. Now, do you have any idea why we have such high variability?

Well, there's some random noise, which we expected, but there are also differences in the work and how it's done. For example, when a small black tote is used, it takes about 8.5 seconds to set up. The bigger grey ones take about 11.5 seconds.

That's a very good observation, but I don't see it on the board. Maybe it could be an observation on the run chart?

You're right. I'll add that now.

Good, remember that we want to have all the relevant information on the board. Let's keep going. What obstacles do you think are preventing you from reaching the target condition?

We have identified nine. We learned in class to note them in the obstacle parking lot so later we can experiment to overcome them one at a time. Let me add that to the board as well.

Very thorough... and which <u>one</u> obstacle are you going to address now?

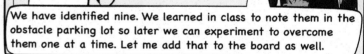

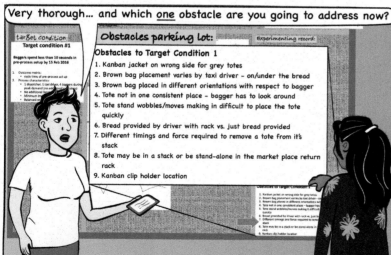

Obstacles parking lot:

Obstacles to Target Condition 1

1. Kanban jacket on wrong side for grey totes
2. Brown bag placement varies by taxi driver - on/under the bread
3. Brown bag placed in different orientations with respect to bagger
4. Tote not in one consistent place - bagger has to look around
5. Tote stand wobbles/moves making in difficult to place the tote quickly
6. Bread provided by driver with rack vs. just bread provided
7. Different timings and force required to remove a tote from it's stack
8. Tote may be in a stack or be stand-alone in the market place return rack
9. Kanban clip holder location

We're thinking of starting with number seven. Totes are kept in a stack, and baggers struggle and waste time trying to separate them.

That's always a pain.

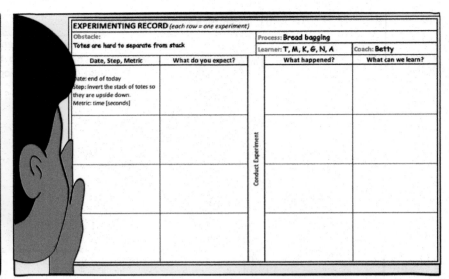

About an hour later...

I'm back. Are you ready for the next coaching cycle?

Of course!

Let's do it, then. What's your challenge?

To process one loaf of bread every 7.5 seconds in December 2016.

That's a very good summary... Can you tell me where we are with respect to the target condition?

Yes. The pre-process setup takes between 5.8 and 17 seconds as you can see on the run chart at the bottom of the board.

Good... what's your target condition?

For baggers to spend less than 10 seconds in pre-process setup while following a clear and repeatable process by 15 Feb 2016.

And what's the actual condition now?

There are three jobs in bread. Bagging is the bottleneck. Besides the actual bagging, they also have setup work for each batch. There's significant... ehh... there's variability in each step, as noted on the block diagram.

Cool. Let's go to the back of the card and find out what you did... What did you plan as your last step?

Reflect on the Last Step Taken
Because you don't actually know what the result of a step will be!

Have the learner state the **obstacle** being worked on

1) What did you plan as your **Last Step**?

2) What did you **Expect**?

3) What **Actually Happened**?

4) What did you **Learn**?

Return to question 3

We planned to invert the stack of totes baggers pull from.

Ok, what did you expect?

To make it easier for baggers to separate the totes and save about two seconds from their pre-process setup.

What actually happened?

There was no improvement. It was just as hard, and the time remained the same.

In fact, it made it worse, since it introduced a possible hygiene issue. The bottom of the totes, now facing up, could get the baggers' hands dirty.

EXPERIMENTING RECORD *(each row = one experiment)*

		Process: **Bread bagging**	
Obstacle:		Learner: **T, M, K, G, N, A**	Coach: **Betty**
Totes are hard to separate from stack			

Date, Step, Metric	What do you expect?		What happened?	What can we learn?
Date: end of today Step: Invert the stack of totes so they are upside down. Metric: time [seconds]	Less effort to separate totes. Faster by 2s.	**Experiment**	Inverting the stack did not make it easier or reduce the time. Moreover, it introduced a hygiene concern as operators would need to touch the bottom of the totes which can be dirty.	1. The 'stickiness' of the totes does not depend on how the totes are stacked. 2. Any solution we consider must maintain the hygienic conditions.
Date: 5 Feb Step: Drill holes in the bottom of the totes. Metric: time [seconds]	Reduced suction between totes. Less effort to separate. Faster by 2s.			

Yes, it was hard not to touch parts of the tote that could be dirty, so baggers would need to change gloves more frequently, resulting in more delays.

Ok. What did you learn?

That the totes are equally hard to separate regardless of how they are stacked, and that we need to ensure hygienic conditions in any experiment that we run.

Good learnings. So, what obstacles do you think are preventing you now from reaching the target condition?

We have not added any new ones... and we're still focusing on the same one—wasted time trying to separate the totes.

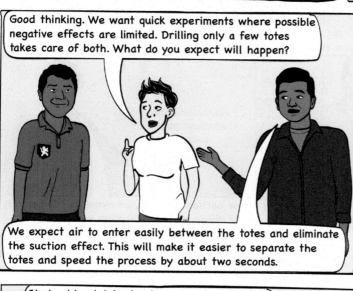

"Hello! I see the whole team is here. Are you ready for the next coaching cycle?"

"We are... we ran our experiment, and the results are in."

"Good. Before we start, I brought J with me today. He's here to help me improve my coaching, so he will mostly observe... but feel free to jump in if I mess up, J. Ready? What's your challenge?"

"By December 2016, bread must be able to process one loaf every 7.5 seconds."

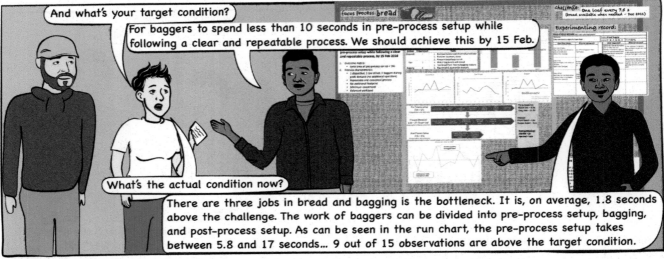

"And what's your target condition?"

"For baggers to spend less than 10 seconds in pre-process setup while following a clear and repeatable process. We should achieve this by 15 Feb."

"What's the actual condition now?"

"There are three jobs in bread and bagging is the bottleneck. It is, on average, 1.8 seconds above the challenge. The work of baggers can be divided into pre-process setup, bagging, and post-process setup. As can be seen in the run chart, the pre-process setup takes between 5.8 and 17 seconds... 9 out of 15 observations are above the target condition."

"Wow, that was great. I have a clear understanding of where you are with respect to your target condition, and you even made the link to the challenge. So, what did you plan as your last step?"

Date, Step, Metric (one experiment)	What do you expect?		What happened?	What can we learn?
Process: Bread bagging				
Learner: T, M, K, G, N, A			**Coach: Betty**	
Date: end of today Step: Invert the stack of totes so they are upside down. Metric: time [seconds]	Less effort to separate totes. Faster by 2s.	Conduct Experiment	Inverting the stack did not make it easier or reduce the time. Moreover, it introduced a hygiene concern as operators would need to touch the bottom of the totes which can be dirty.	1. The 'stickiness' of the totes does not depend on how the totes are stacked. 2. Any solution we consider must maintain the hygienic conditions.
Date: 5 Feb Step: Drill holes in the bottom of the totes. Metric: time [seconds]	Reduced suction between totes. Less effort to separate. Faster by 2s.		There was no notable improvement in effort or time to separate the totes.	Suction between the totes does not seem to be what keeps them together. The totes are tall, so it's probably the friction along the sides.
Date: 10 Feb Step: Have the taxi driver deliver individual totes to the baggers. Metric: time [seconds]	Reduced workload for baggers. Faster by 4+ s. Taxi driver's workload remains under 7.5s.			

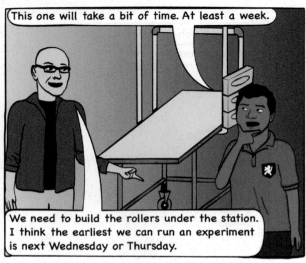

Let me interrupt here. We just went through a series of coaching cycles, with each one building on the learnings from the previous one. This continued through the rest of the semester. I want to highlight a few key points:

1. You can distinguish two loops in Kata. A larger one, defined by the 4 steps of the Improvement Kata, and the shorter PDCA cycles of each experiment: plan the next step, define what to expect, run the experiment, examine the results, and reflect.

2. These two loops define the pattern of scientific thinking we want people to learn. As coaches, we need to help learners develop clear connections within and between loops. For example, at ZMO, we found it useful to start coaching cycles by asking about the challenge, to bring the learners to the larger loop before they plunge into the PDCA cycle.

3. The Kata story board reinforces a scientific thinking pattern and helps make visible the invisible thinking of the learner, so the coach can give fitting feedback. The learner updates it before each coaching cycle to tell a compelling and logically sound story linking all elements of both Kata loops.

4. Coaching in Kata is not about telling people what to do; it's about guiding them through questions so they figure things out by themselves. The questions on the card are headings, and the coach often has to add clarifying questions to recognize where the learner is in their understanding of Kata and challenge them to think deeply about their assumptions, logic being followed, and understanding of the process being improved. But the learner needs to remain in control, which creates much higher engagement and ownership.

BETTY: Good points Tom. It's easy to get good at reciting the five questions, but there's more to coaching scientific thinking than just that. This earlier version of the coaching card can help us see the questions more as headings for guiding learners as they explore. It's from Mike Rother's research looking at Toyota managers.

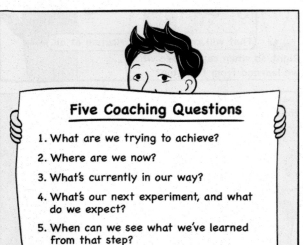

Five Coaching Questions

1. What are we trying to achieve?

2. Where are we now?

3. What's currently in our way?

4. What's our next experiment, and what do we expect?

5. When can we see what we've learned from that step?

I learned a lot from Tilo Schwarz, who taught me about asking deepening questions when the learner can't really answer a question precisely. The deepening question might get the learner to, well, go deeper, like describing the 'condition' part of a target condition instead of just the desired numerical outcome.

Tilo focuses on developing coaches and teaches them to not just rush through the questions.

Here's a great bit of advice I got from him. After the learner provides an answer to each question, think of a traffic light. Go on green for a good answer and stop on red for one that's not precise enough. Ask deepening questions at that point, to help the learner clarify for themselves what they know and, especially, what they don't know.

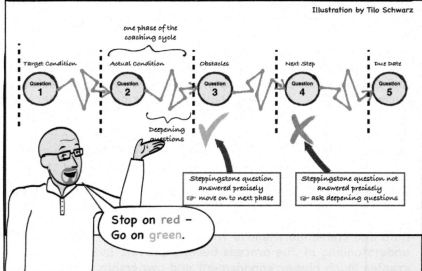

Illustration by Tilo Schwarz

Stop on red –
Go on green.

44

That's what we call finding the 'threshold of knowledge' (TOK). When you find a TOK in your coaching conversation there's not much point in speculating. Instead, go right to question 4 and ask the learner about their next step for finding out what they don't yet know!

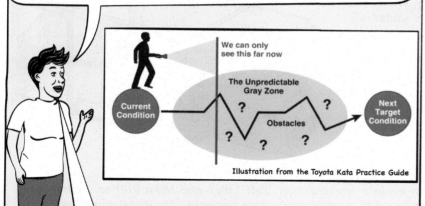

Illustration from the Toyota Kata Practice Guide

Sometimes a learner will be hesitant to admit they don't know the answer, especially at the start. You can make them feel more comfortable not knowing by saying question 4 this way: "Don't worry if you don't know. What is your next step to find out?"

Help your learner plan a next experiment that can be done quickly, cheaply, and safely.

Note that the coach is practicing new skills too, which means both persons are learners. Because of that a real relationship begins to form, characterized by trust and humility.

TOM

Let's go back to our story now... In case you're wondering, the experiment worked beautifully. We ended up installing rollers under all bread stations.

Thanks to the quick mocked-up experiment, the team had time to tackle another obstacle. This allowed them to achieve the target condition by the due date. Rapid experimentation increases the rate of improvement and learning, and frequent repetition is the most effective way to build the habit of thinking scientifically.

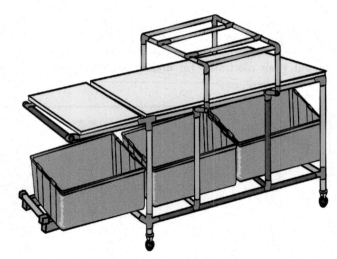

At the end of the semester, each team made a presentation. Jeff Liker and Mike Rother attended and provided feedback. It was a great finale to a very productive semester for developing the students, our people, and ZMO in general. Let's take a quick look as the bread team closes their presentation.

I would like to leave you with a quick summary of what our team accomplished. We went through two target conditions, tackled eight obstacles, and ran 21 experiments. As you can see in the run charts, we reached both target conditions.

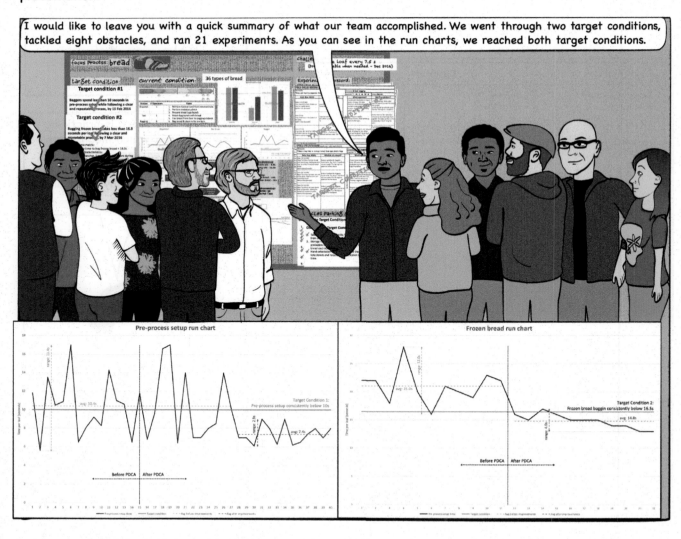

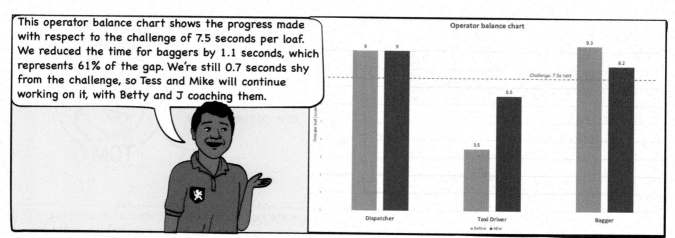

This operator balance chart shows the progress made with respect to the challenge of 7.5 seconds per loaf. We reduced the time for baggers by 1.1 seconds, which represents 61% of the gap. We're still 0.7 seconds shy from the challenge, so Tess and Mike will continue working on it, with Betty and J coaching them.

Operator balance chart

Challenge: 7.5s takt

Dispatcher: 9, 9
Taxi Driver: 3.5, 6.5
Bagger: 9.3, 8.2

Before / After

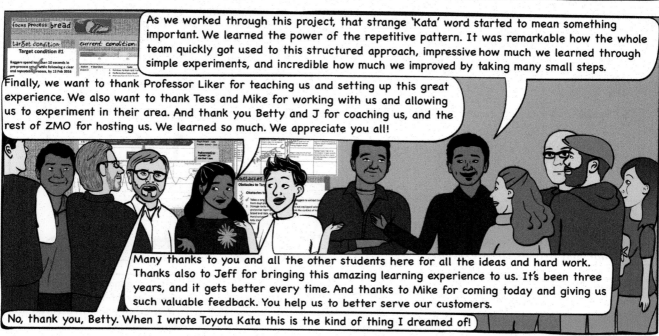

As we worked through this project, that strange 'Kata' word started to mean something important. We learned the power of the repetitive pattern. It was remarkable how the whole team quickly got used to this structured approach, impressive how much we learned through simple experiments, and incredible how much we improved by taking many small steps.

Finally, we want to thank Professor Liker for teaching us and setting up this great experience. We also want to thank Tess and Mike for working with us and allowing us to experiment in their area. And thank you Betty and J for coaching us, and the rest of ZMO for hosting us. We learned so much. We appreciate you all!

Many thanks to you and all the other students here for all the ideas and hard work. Thanks also to Jeff for bringing this amazing learning experience to us. It's been three years, and it gets better every time. And thanks to Mike for coming today and giving us such valuable feedback. You help us to better serve our customers.

No, thank you, Betty. When I wrote Toyota Kata this is the kind of thing I dreamed of!

The ZMO leadership team held a reflection meeting to celebrate their success, identify some key learnings, and think about next steps.

Let's look in on the conversation. TOM

I have not been involved with Kata much, but there's no doubt it has been a success. Can someone explain why this is?

With Kata, anyone can learn to think scientifically. The only requirement is a commitment to learn by actual practice! It is not just a theoretical exercise.

For me, Kata has made real the idea of developing people as we improve the process by solving problems. It provides a structured approach that, through repetition, develops the pattern of scientific thinking. Once you get it, it becomes part of how you think, and continuous improvement becomes a reality beyond the formal Kata project.

There's no end to people's creativity when the culture and systems allow them to develop.

Very true. I'm frequently surprised by the ideas our people have and by how much we as managers have learned. When we introduced Kata, we were looking for a way to engage the crew. It took a while for us to realize we were all learning scientific thinking, and that would be the true power of Kata.

Good point, but let's talk about this engagement you were looking for, which I think is one of the most interesting aspects of Kata. Perhaps it's the structured process, the easy to understand steps, its action orientation toward quick experimentation, or being able to see progress toward the challenge... whatever it is, Kata brought a level of engagement and ownership that only the leaders had before.

I think all those things contribute. Remember when we asked the crew about it? Some mentioned the process helped them structure their thinking, some liked the clear direction and focus, others liked seeing the progress they were making... someone even mentioned feeling in control.

For me, perhaps the biggest difference Kata has made is that I don't feel I must have answers for everything.

Having a common language and way of thinking about problems has also made a difference. People feel empowered because now they can discuss problems and solutions on equal footing with anyone in the organization.

What do you mean? That's part of your job description. Didn't you read the fine print?

It certainly seemed that way. As a manager and ZMO veteran, people expect me to know stuff. They think I should be able to answer and solve everything on the spot. Before Kata, I also thought this was my job. Now I feel comfortable saying "I don't know, but I know a process we can use to figure it out together." It's liberating!

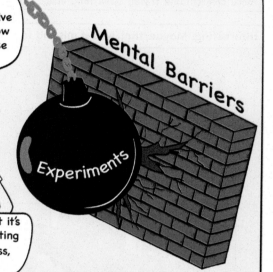

Mental Barriers

Experiments

I also like that, Betty. For me, there's one more thing, but at the moment it's more a hypothesis than a conclusion. I believe Kata's focus on experimenting toward a clear goal removes mental barriers that normally block progress, and also promotes perseverance to keep trying until success is achieved.

What do you mean by removing mental barriers?

I can see that. If you tell me to change how I do something, the first reaction I'll have is to think of all the reasons why your method won't work and how it will make my life worse.

Well, I think people are more receptive to new ideas they see as experiments. If it does not work, we learn and try again. The first 'solution' does not have to be permanent. Second and third chances are allowed, and even encouraged. Talking about permanent change tends to raise all kinds of barriers.

Exactly! So we start off on the wrong foot. And I think that ties directly to perseverance. Say I convince you to implement one of these permanent solutions, but it does not perform as expected. What would you do?

I would probably revert to my old process and ignore your suggestions in the future.

Sure, I would too. Now, what if we try the exact same change, but instead I tell you we're going to run an experiment, learn from it, and based on that, figure out what to do next... what would you do if the idea fails?

I would feel more in control and would be more comfortable trying something else.

There you go... and we get perseverance to see improvements through. We often think perseverance is a fixed personality trait you have to hire for. But maybe it can grow from using Kata. I think this is a key strength of scientific thinking, and of Kata in particular. Just focusing on running experiments instead of implementing solutions makes a huge difference.

Hmm... perhaps you're onto something here.

Interesting. Maybe that was a missing ingredient in all the problem-solving tools we tried.

We thought a 'rigorous' problem-solving method and incentives was the key, but people felt the opposite of efficacy.

With the grants it was all about money and we lost any sense of satisfaction.

I think we're learning that if people understand the problem and direction and are coached on how to test their ideas, they get engaged. That was our goal from the start.

Prof. Liker

How do you create alignment across your organization? How do you get team members more actively engaged with improving the work?

The ZMO teams achieved great improvement results, but more importantly their thinking shifted to a more exploratory scientific outlook, which in turn grew their confidence to tackle challenges. The successes build efficacy that makes you want to play again, and even some failures keep up the challenge and interest, kind of like a video game.

Practicing the behaviors of scientific thinking develops neurological pathways – habits – that make us more engaged problem solvers.

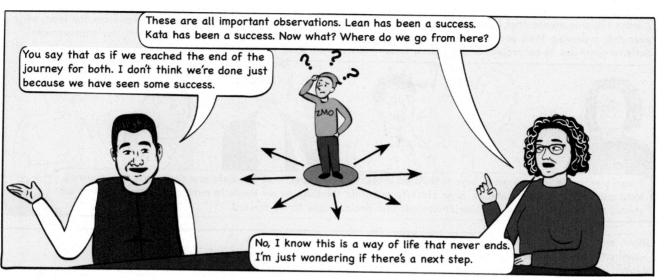

These are all important observations. Lean has been a success. Kata has been a success. Now what? Where do we go from here?

You say that as if we reached the end of the journey for both. I don't think we're done just because we have seen some success.

No, I know this is a way of life that never ends. I'm just wondering if there's a next step.

I would say we continue with the same approach. Solve problems to pull improvements and develop people. The focus will depend on the specific issues we're facing, no?

Well, I think Kata may be able to help here. Remember step one – define the direction. Wouldn't it be better to pull improvements as we move in the direction of a challenge?

1

Set the Direction or Challenge

2 Grasp the Current Condition

3 Establish your Next Target Condition

4 Conduct Experiments to get there

Good point! Kata starts with a clear direction, but how do we identify the critical challenges that will define it? We may have to go beyond Kata for this. Toyota has a planning process to develop a long-term vision and an annual plan at all levels. It's this Hoshin Kanri, or policy deployment, we have talked about. Maybe it is time to think beyond individual Kata projects and shoot for true widespread continuous improvement.

But we have been talking about all the involvement we have gotten by using Kata. Is that not enough?

VISION

HOSHIN KANRI

Break down problems

Individual contribution

Vertical alignment

Horizontal alignment

Company Hoshin

Department Hoshin

Individual Hoshin

ACT PLAN CHECK DO

I think Eduardo means that Kata increased participation and engagement greatly, but we're still far from the ideal of everyone improving their processes every day, together, toward a common vision. For the most part, our improvement activity continues to be project based. Run a Kata here or run a Kata there.

I agree with the idea of going beyond isolated projects. Remember that the Kata are really practice routines. Mike calls them Starter Kata... a jump start to scientific thinking. As we begin to naturally think that way, we should mature to a system of clear challenges and goals people strive toward.

Right, and I think ZMO is strongest at a middle level, where improvement is based on projects focused on specific processes. This includes the Kata activity as well as the efforts we make as we strive to improve flow. We're weaker at both a higher level of bigger, longer, top-driven projects that tie directly to the long-term vision, and at a lower level where everyone makes small improvements to their processes every day.

Long-term projects

✓ Specific-process Kata projects

Everyday small improvements

For the top side, we have already had a few discussions and agreed to experiment with Hoshin Kanri at the warehouse next year.

Hoshin Kanri should help define priorities for this group. And, by cascading down clear objectives for specific areas and people, it should help us generate challenges for Kata projects that are well aligned with the long-term vision.

Hoshin Kanri

Long-term projects

Specific-process Kata projects

Everyday small improvements

But what drives the bottom level?

Well, I think Kata plays a role there as well, but perhaps not with structured projects. What we need is for people to apply the scientific thinking they learn from Kata, to their everyday experience.

The theory sounds good, but how do we do this in practice?

But won't we get more of a scattershot approach this way? One of the advantages of Kata is focus. Won't we lose some of that?

Well, the True North should help align efforts with our general direction, and Hoshin Kanri provides clear goals. Besides, I don't think scattershot improvement is inherently bad... and in fact, it may be needed for true widespread continuous improvement. A good blend of intentional improvement toward clear goals, and just solving small issues people face every day, may prove to be the right mix. The problem is not a scattershot approach but who is involved in it.

I don't have all the answers, but I think an element we're missing is a clear direction. Toyota uses the idea of producing one-by-one, in sequence, on demand, with zero waste as a guiding force. If we define a True North that is simple and enduring, we can give people a direction that they can use as the starting point to apply the scientific thinking they have learned.

Hoshin Kanri	Long-term projects
	Specific-process Kata projects
True North	Everyday small improvements

What do you mean?

Well, anyone in this group that spends time on improvement should focus on critical ZMO issues. Take capacity. Your effort should be focused on the bottleneck. However, captains should work constantly on increasing efficiency in their areas, and the crew should be improving their stations and processes every day, even if they are nowhere near the bottleneck.

I had not thought about it in that way. So everyone should be improving, but their focus depends on their area of influence.

Right. A captain improving a non-bottleneck area is not lacking focus. On the contrary, it's a lost opportunity if they are not doing it. The chance the bread captain will drive improvements at the bottleneck in check are slim to none. So why not have them improve their area? Perhaps they will stay ahead of demand growth and never become the bottleneck.

Let me see if I got this right. Hoshin Kanri helps the leadership team focus on critical issues and helps define challenges for Kata projects. Those Kata projects drive needed improvements and develop scientific thinking. But we also want a lot of other improvements in the direction of this True North, even if they do not directly relate to the defined challenges. For this, the crew uses the scientific thinking they learn through Kata.

Perfect. But this is an experiment, so now we have to try it out and see what we learn.

Am I hearing another meta-experiment with us as guinea pigs?

At least this one I know about!

We're all together in this one. At least around here I will be a well-fed guinea pig.

Good! We have learned a lot today and we even have a direction to continue evolving. Anything else?

Just one more thing... here's to the next 15 years of experiments and surprises!

Eduardo Lander

Jeffrey Liker

Tom Root

A Note From the Authors

Now you have seen Toyota Kata at work. Managers coached ZMO associates, and university students, on projects to practice scientific thinking. Associates who had little interest in or exposure to science were suddenly observing and measuring the current condition, forming hypothesis, running experiments, and were for the first time highly engaged.

We talk a lot about engagement but that often leads to platitudes. "Give people a why for their engagement." "Explain what is in it for them." "Reward them for good ideas." "Eliminate fear of failure." "Show appreciation." "Actively listen."

These are all very reasonable, except they do not work. Of course, if you give employees money for ideas, or set a quota for a minimum number per month, you will get ideas. But will they be good ones? Will they address critical issues? Will employees have any real stake in the outcome?

What we have illustrated with the Improvement Kata and Coaching Kata is something different.

> What? There was a clear goal of the skill we wanted people to develop—a scientific thinking mindset, to learn our way toward solving complex problems and achieving meaningful goals.
> Why? Scientific thinking is the best way we know to navigate through uncertainty and achieve wildly important goals for the individual and organization.
> How? The Improvement Kata model is a clear and simple pattern for how to work scientifically toward challenges.
> How? Changing habitual ways of thinking requires new habits achieved through deliberate practice.
> How? A coach helps guide the learner, through corrective feedback often in the form of questions, rather than advice or answers.
> How? Starter Kata are practiced by both the learner and coach, that is, small practice routines for different elements of the Improvement Kata model.

ZMO management was able to provide a structure for daily learning, help identify important goals, and personally lead by coaching. It certainly helped that ZMO is highly people centered and even has gainsharing so associates participate in the profits of the business.

We also saw what did not work: paying people to learn to solve problems, trying to use complex problem-solving methods with a lot of front-end analysis before getting to trying things, and management doing the main thinking and then inviting ideas from associates.

Managers at ZMO had been practicing Lean for years, but they realized this was different and started as learners rather than jumping right to being coaches. They soon found that they also benefited from practicing scientific thinking with the Improvement Kata and were learning at least as much as the associates.

What you hold in your hands is a real story with many positive consequences for the people at ZMO and their customers. We hope that presenting it as a comic helped you connect to the real-life characters.

Now it's your turn. What have you learned from this case example? Can you imagine benefits of scientific thinking? If so, get started now. Find a coach. It does not need to be an expert. You can struggle and learn together. Coach each other. Pick an important problem, personal or professional. Define a wildly important challenge. Experiment. Here's the 'Kata Code':

1) Conditions are unpredictable.
2) Enjoy the learning zone.
3) Understand the direction,
    grasp the current condition,
    establish a target condition,
    experiment toward the target condition.
4) Beginners practice Starter Kata exactly.
5) Have a coach, be a coach.

Toyota Kata and the focus on scientific thinking were the result of six years of research by our colleague Mike Rother. In fact, it was Mike's idea to do an additional graphic novel focusing on TK and he did a rough mockup and added his ideas and creativity throughout the book. Mike did not want any recognition and instead explained that supporting people in sharing what they are learning about Toyota Kata and scientific thinking is his role, so that this young topic can grow and evolve in ways we might not imagine. Not just for operations improvement or even just the business world, but for anyone finding their way through the zone of uncertainty to any complex goal. This one is for you.

Thank you for joining us. We were fans of comics growing up and had a blast making our own, and hope you enjoyed it too!

ADDENDUM

Before we go, here's a closer look at some of the Toyota Kata 'Starter Kata' practice routines we used in this story. You'll find them useful for your practice of scientific thinking.

BETTY

The Five Coaching Kata Questions
(Turn the card over to reflect on the last step)

COACHING KATA

The Five Questions
1. What is the **Target Condition**?
2. What is the **Actual Condition** now?
--------(Turn Card Over)------------->
3. What **Obstacles** do you think are preventing you from reaching the target condition? Which *one* are you addressing now?
4. What is your **Next Step**? (Next experiment) What do you expect?
5. How quickly can we go and see what we **Have Learned** from taking that step?

*You'll often work on the same obstacle with several experiments

Reflect on the Last Step Taken
Because you don't actually know what the result of a step will be!

Have the learner state the obstacle being worked on
1. What did you plan as your **Last Step**?
2. What did you **Expect**?
3. What **Actually Happened**?
4. What did you **Learn**?

-------------------------------->
Return to question 3

Purpose of asking the 5 questions:

- Reinforce the scientific pattern of the Improvement Kata.

- Help the coach see how the learner is thinking, so the coach can give appropriate feedback.

The 5 questions are the headings for each coaching cycle

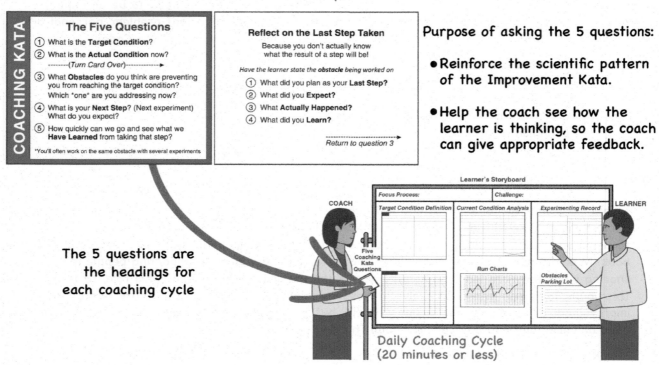

Learner's Storyboard

COACH
Five Coaching Kata Questions

Focus Process:
Challenge:

Target Condition Definition | Current Condition Analysis | Experimenting Record

Run Charts

Obstacles Parking Lot

LEARNER

Daily Coaching Cycle
(20 minutes or less)

Learner's Storyboard

The learner's storyboard is the communication point between the coach and the learner.

Focus Process:		Challenge: What we want to achieve	
Target Condition Achieve by: _____	**Current Condition**	**Experimenting Record**	
Where we want to be next (Typically 2 weeks out)	Where we are today	Experiments (Against obstacles and toward the target condition)	
		Obstacles Parking Lot List of perceived obstacles to the target condition (Work on one at a time)	

The Starter Kata images on these pages are from the Toyota Kata Practice Guide.

Here are copier templates for the five question card and the experimenting record.

TOM

Front of card

COACHING KATA

The Five Questions

① What is the **Target Condition**?

② What is the **Actual Condition** now?

--------(*Turn Card Over*)-------------→

③ What **Obstacles** do you think are preventing you from reaching the target condition?

Which *one* are you addressing now?

④ What is your **Next Step**? (Next experiment) What do you expect?

⑤ How quickly can we go and see what we **Have Learned** from taking that step?

*You'll often work on the same obstacle with several experiments

Back of card

Reflect on the Last Step Taken

Because you don't actually know
what the result of a step will be!

*Have the learner state the **obstacle** being worked on*

① What did you plan as your **Last Step?**

② What did you **Expect?**

③ What **Actually Happened?**

④ What did you **Learn?**

------------------------------→

Return to question 3

EXPERIMENTING RECORD *(Each row = one experiment)*

Obstacle:

Process:

Learner: **Coach:**

Date & step	What do you expect + metric	Conduct the Experiment / Do a Coaching Cycle	What happened	What we learned

Eduardo Lander is Founder of Custom Lean Systems and Founding Partner of Dobilo. He has been studying Lean since 1995. As a plant manager, learning from books and through trial and error; as a Doctor of Engineering student under Jeff Liker at the University of Michigan; from inside Toyota, working in the Chief Engineer function at Toyota Motor Europe; and as a consultant, working mostly with companies dealing with high variability. He now supports Lean transformations by helping organizations improve their processes and develop their people using Lean principles and Toyota Kata.

Jeffrey K. Liker is Professor Emeritus, Industrial and Operations Engineering at The University of Michigan and President of Liker Lean Advisors, LLC. He is author of the best-selling book, The Toyota Way, Second Edition, and has coauthored nine other books about Toyota including The Toyota Way to Service Excellence, Designing the Future, and The Toyota Way to Lean Leadership. With Tilo Schwarz, he wrote Giving Wings to Her Team: A Novel about Learning to Coach the Toyota Kata Way. His articles and books have won thirteen Shingo Prizes for Research Excellence. He was inducted into the Association of Manufacturing Excellence Hall of Fame and the Shingo Academy.

Tom Root is Managing Partner of Zingerman's Mail Order and Co-Founder of Maker Works in Ann Arbor MI. He has taught and practiced Lean principles for 15 years as Partner/Owner at Zingerman's Mail Order, in the Zingerman's Community of Businesses as Chief Operating Officer, and as a lecturer at the University of Michigan.